I0430201

TABLE OF CONTENTS

INTRODUCTION

Growth and development of new nations often results in conflict among peoples vying for the occupation of the same land. Although the American Indian was the original inhabitant of North America, his society was eventually subordinated to the extent of a second rate population. Following colonial establishment in America, the European Colonialists continued to expand their territory, shaping the political and cultural environment to their advantage. This entire period of expansionism is a somewhat neglected part of American History, with respect to the Indian, in which our founding father's ideologies and initiative to develop the United States of America into a continental nation facilitated the commission of acts against the Cherokee Indian that would be considered genocidal actions according to the presently accepted definition.

The following chapters will explain the genesis of the term genocide, present the widely accepted formal definition, as well as illustrate examples of the characteristics of genocide. Further, the text will exemplify the trials and tribulations of the Cherokee Indian in their effort with the United States government to gain and maintain sovereignty. Unaccusingly and without desire for retribution, the collective experience of this work will show evidence that through the natural growth of the United States certain actions were taken against the Cherokee Indian, during the period of 1785 to 1907, that would be considered unacceptable in the present day climate of the media microscope.

To better understand the process of how this came to fruition there is need to gain the perspective of the people involved at the onset of the process. As European nations began to explore and discover new lands they derived the need to avoid wars of ownership in their new lands. According to Historian Jack Utter, the prevailing thought was based largely on the premise that the Pope provided the authority to possess the lands without regard for native populations. As time passed the Pope's international authority began to diminish. Thus arouse the need for another policy. That policy was found to be the Doctrine of Discovery. This doctrine legalized the right to claim title to lands as long as the founder maintained a presence within the boundaries of the claimed area.[1]

The United States sanctioned this discovery doctrine in 1823. In the Supreme Court case of Johnson and Graham's Lessee v. William McIntosh a dispute over land title was judged. This case articulated the nature of Indian land title under the United States.[2] The following excerpt illustrates the view of the United States of the legal effect of the discovery doctrine established by the Europeans:

> While the different nations of Europe respected the right of the Natives, as occupants, they asserted the ultimate domination to be in themselves; and claimed and exercised, as a consequence of this ultimate dominion, a power to grant the soil, while yet in the possession of the Natives. These grants have been understood by all, to convey a title to the grantees, subject only to the Indian right to occupancy. [For which some form of compensation was usually paid.]
>
> No one of the powers of Europe gave its full assent to this principle, more unequivocally than England. The documents upon this subject are ample and complete.
>
> Thus, all the nations of Europe, who have acquired territory on this continent, have asserted in themselves, and have recognized in others, the exclusive right of the discoverer to appropriate the lands occupied by the Indians. Have the American States adopted or rejected this principle?
>
> By the treaty which concluded the war of our revolution, Great Britain relinquished all claim, not only to the government, but to the 'property and territorial rights of the United States,'....By this treaty, the powers of government, and the right to the soil, which had previously been in Great Britain, passed definitely to these States.
>
> The United States, then, have unequivocally acceded to that great and broad rule by which its civilized inhabitants now hold this country. They hold, and assert themselves, the title by which it is acquired. They maintain, as all others have maintained, that discovery gave an exclusive right to extinguish the Indian title of occupancy, either by purchase or by conquest; and gave also a right to such a degree of sovereignty [over Indians and their land], as the circumstances of the people [of the U.S.] would allow them to exercise.[3]

Why would a student of military history be interested in reading a paper about genocide? The term genocide, and its application, appears to be developing into a vogue term in the current century. Since its coining and acceptance as a crime following World War II, there has been

---

[1] Jack Utter, *American Indians: Answers to Today's Questions* (Lake Ann: National Woodlands Publishing Company, 1993), 6-7.

[2] Francis Paul Prucha, *Documents of United States Indian Policy*, 3rd ed. (Lincoln and London: University of Nebraska Press, 2000), 35.

[3] Jack Utter, *American Indians: Answers to Today's Questions* (Lake Ann: National Woodlands Publishing Company, 1993), 7-8.

increasing awareness and outcry as nationalism is on the rise throughout the global community. Military leadership at all levels of war should be familiar with the term, how to recognize the patterns that result in genocide, and how it might impact upon mission accomplishment. As ambassadors of our Nation, military leaders must also understand United States history as it influences the perception of our government as viewed from foreign nations. Lastly, by understanding genocide, future military leadership will be able to conduct and articulate the purpose of operations throughout the spectrum of warfare while remaining disassociated with the negative connotations surrounding genocidal activities.

NAMING THE ATROCITY

Acts of aggression and brutality have been a part of mankind since the beginning of time. Man was created with a free will that drives him to interact and manipulate the environment surrounding him. In that environment are other humans which, according to history, man has developed the need to project his will upon the wills of others. Too often is the case when the imposition of one's will is expressed in a destructive form. What exactly do we call this phenomenon? This section will explain the origin of the term genocide, describe several characteristics of the term and then explain how the international community has defined genocide in the twentieth century.

ORIGIN

As is common with most words of the contemporary English language, its root can be traced back to the Greek and Latin language. Genocide originates from the Greek *genos*, meaning "race," "nation," or "tribe," and the Latin *cide*, meaning "killing." Dr. Raphael Lemkin coined the term in 1943 after events in Europe demanded terminology for the deliberate destruction of large groups of people. Up to this period terms such as "denationalization" and "Germanization" had been used to describe the atrocity but they did "not adequately convey the full force of the new phenomenon of genocide. They signify only the substitution of the national pattern of the oppressor for the original national pattern but not the destruction of the biological and physical structure of the oppressed group."[4] David Stannard provides a further illustration of Dr. Lemkin's thought process:

> Under Lemkin's definition, genocide was the coordinated and planned annihilation of a national, religious, or racial group by a variety of actions aimed at undermining the foundations essential to the survival of the group as a group. Lemkin conceived of

---

[4] Ralph Lemkin, "Genocide - A Modern Crime," Free World (New York), Vol. 9, No. 4, April 1945, http://www.preventgenocide.org/lemkin/freeworld1945.htm, accessed 12 December 2001.

genocide as "a composite of different acts persecution or destruction." His definition included attacks on political and social institutions, culture, language, national feelings, religion, and the economic existence of the group. Even nonlethal acts that undermined the liberty, dignity, and personal security of members of a group constituted genocide if they contributed to weakening the viability of the group. Under Lemkin's definition, acts of ethnocide—a term coined by the French after the war to cover the destruction of a culture without the killing of its bearers—also qualified as genocide.[5]

CHARACTERISTICS

Part of understanding the term is the capability to recognize the characteristics of genocide. The results of genocide, unfortunately, are painfully obvious and should be avoided by civilized nations. Thus it is important to recognize the characteristics that underpin the evolutionary approach to genocide. Because genocide is not a naturally occurring phenomenon in any species but man, the characteristics reside in, or are linked to, the psychological makeup of individuals or groups. The following text will provide insight into the characteristics of dehumanization, individual experience, group experience, and the role of leaders. Any one of these characteristics can singularly or collectively be found in the ingredients of genocide.

In order to gain a perspective on dehumanization first consider the dynamic of the familiar and unfamiliar. Everyone knows the comfort or security they feel in the familiar surroundings of family members, friends or neighbors. All of these individuals are people with occupations, goals, dreams, and loved ones. Typically they interact on a regular basis, are involved in each other's lives and would go to any length to assist the needy party in the time of want. This feeling of familiarity is a source of strength and reassurance. When people are in a familiar environment they are not likely to aggressively act out against one another.

On a different note, in the unfamiliar environment susceptibility and apprehensiveness

---

[5] David E.Stannard, *American Holocaust: The Conquest of the New World* (New York: Oxford University Press, 1992), 279.

replace the feeling of security. To be cast into the company of a stranger creates one level of anxiety while the accompaniment of strangers vastly different, as in race and ethnicity elevates that anxiety to an even higher level. People do not feel the bond with strangers and thus will not respond to them as they do those that are familiar to them. Normally the needs of the stranger do not bear the same weight as those close. This is why humans are able to disassociate themselves from tragedies that happen to other people. An example of this is when an individual listens to a news broadcast about the murder of a stranger. There is no emotional attachment as long as one does not know the other person.

Dehumanization

During times of war the propaganda machine capitalizes on the differences of strangers to empower people to carry out their aggression against the enemy; or in other words, to facilitate the killing or destruction of the enemy. Propaganda attempts to demonize or dehumanize the enemy. If another group of people is visualized as inferior, or possibly even not human, people can more easily impose their will upon them. This conception of strangers can easily facilitate violence. Dehumanization is an important psychological step that enables normal people to justify, in their own minds, that violent action against the lesser individual is acceptable. Israel Charney further states that, "What human beings do through the enormous power of symbolization (or ideology) is to redefine another people as not of our species and then set them up as subject to that natural aspect of animal life that permits violence against strangers or members of another species more readily than against member of one's own family or species."[6]

The recent history of the United States holds several illustrations of aggressive uprising spurred by the differences of strangers within and exterior to the borders of the country. Nearly

---

[6] Israel W. Charney, *How Can We Commit the Unthinkable? Genocide: The Human Cancer* (Boulder: Westview Press, Inc., 1982) 190.

everyone is familiar with the terms "nips," "gooks," "niggers," or "ragheads" and the emotions they evoke within people. Any one of these terms causes people to align or disassociate themselves according to the labels and find adequate excuse for killing or some other form of aggression. This division of people according to their natural differences and the developed hatred fueled by dehumanization is one reason that facilitates war and possible genocide.[7]

Individual Experience

Is the normal human capable of being a genocider? It is typical to call genociders "madmen". Many would say that Adoplh Hilter could easily be labeled as such. One may also suggest that any one of us is capable of attaining similar notoriety depending on his/her individual experience. On the individual basis the tendency to project aggression against others often develops over an extensive period of time. For example, many analogies are drawn about how violent video games lead children to the propensity to kill each other in their own school yards; or how the adult pornography industry encourages the dehumanization of women, thus leading men to devalue them which leads to crime against women. Israel Charney brings this individual experience to an even simpler form by explaining,

> The dehumanization process extends along a continuum to the ultimate of removing the other person's opportunity to live. The "little" everyday dehumanizations we practice on one another are stations on the way toward the ultimate act of one person taking away another's life. It is not simply the insult that we do to another that is at stake in everyday dehumanizations. Its is the fact that we are learning a devastating process, rehearsing it deriving gratification from it, and perhaps preparing ourselves to one day participate in the removal of other people's lives.[8]

Certainly most people experience thoughts, if not active insults about others on occasion. Fortunately for most, a system of personal checks and balances exists to prevent the escalation to violence projection.

---

[7] Charney, 190.
[8] Charney, 207.

A second aspect that can find the normal human in the unacceptable position as the destructor is the occasion when the destruction is the result of unintended circumstances. Impulsive is defined as actuated or swayed by emotional or involuntary impulse. Often times people acting impulsively in the heat of the moment unintentionally do things that harm other people whether they are victims or simply innocent bystanders. Israel Charney explains:

> People also fear unintentional destructiveness, and with good reason. The very power we develop for our lives is potentially explosive and destructive. Moreover, there is much that we do not know about how to store, transmit, and channel our power. The basic problem is that it is in the nature of power—when expressed or directed toward others—to press, penetrate and ultimately attack, hurt and fell. It is in the nature of power to be what it is by virtue of nothing more than the momentum of the thrust of energy. In other words, even though one may not want to kill, a powerful charge of strength aimed at another *can* kill. Small everyday examples of men "killing" each other without wanting to are to be found in business and career struggles. One may intend to succeed in one's own career without pushing others aside, but the sheer flow of competitive effort may very well find one bringing other's careers to a halt.
>
> It is also in the nature of power to be destructive of another when the other person is unable to stand up against the energy directed at him and deflect, absorb, or transform the energy for his own use. There are any number of tragic situations in which a blow that is intended to be far less damaging than it proves to be destroys another person, not because the destruction is willed on any level of conscious or unconscious desire, but because the power unleashed is too great for the recipient to manage. Some moments of unplanned violence take place in great rushes of impulsiveness. "My God, I killed him; I didn't mean to." Other incidents of unplanned violence occur because of remarkably poor, but fundamentally innocent, judgement. "We were playing with the gun. I was sure it was unloaded, but when I aimed it at him and fired, he let out a gasp and fell."[9]

Another source of destructiveness comes from power. The local schoolhouse Bully derives great pleasure from imposing his will or exerting his power over his schoolmates. Typically he acts out in order to make up for his own shortcomings, because he refuses to see a situation from any ones else's perspective, he enjoys abusing others to get what he wants, or to demonstrate that he is stronger than every one else.

---

[9] Charney, 64.

8

The bully typically rejects established rules and regulations in his rebellion, which fuels his need for a feeling of security and supremacy.[10]

The limited training individuals receive in making choices also influences human destructiveness. Ponder the concept of means and ends. The ends represent the goals people choose for themselves. The means represent the manner in which those ends or goals are achieved. Israel Charney points out that when people are confronted with decisions, they typically choose the status quo and continue to march. This way they can more easily avoid the anxiety of failure through the security of doing things the way everyone else does. Since the decision was based on status quo vice true desire, the viability of not seeing the decision through to fruition often is countered with an effort similar to that of a Nazi trying to deny his Jewish heritage. In the same fashion, people are not taught how to choose the means in which their goal will be accomplished.[11] Mathematics shows that the shortest distance between two points is a straight line. Too often choices are made in the initial stages of a plan that fail to contemplate the adverse repercussions of the plan. This can easily be seen in the implications that arose from the production of nuclear power at Chernobyl, Russia. No one thought that disaster was going to happen, but the decision to produce the nuclear power without an adequate response measure in place was made.

Lastly at the individual experience level is the concept of denial. Denial can be thought of as a passive form of destructiveness. Denying the fact that hurtful things have taken place does not make them go away. In fact, it often allows them to continue unimpeded. As long as the violence is occurring to a remote person it is easy to convince

---

[10] Charney, 65.
[11] Charney, 96.

oneself that it is not taking place. Why do humans choose not to recognize the violence? Israel Charney suggests that there are two reasons:

1. Society denies the fact that the atrocities are occurring because they believe that any action taken by them will not be able to influence the eventual outcome. Since the belief is that nothing can be done, people generally find it more pleasing to simply pretend that the condition does not exist.

2. Humans tend to refuse to acknowledge the violence because it exemplifies their inner destructiveness. Most people have experienced fleeting ideas of violence but never act upon them. We grow up being taught that violence, particularly against humans, is part of a demented dark world that is undesirable with which to be associated. When confronted or placed in a situation where those inner destructive thoughts might be revealed, people protect themselves by remaining as remote as possible from any association of their personality with the darkness of violence.[12] David Stannard puts a slightly different twist to the reasoning for denial in that:

> Denial of massive death counts is common—and even readily understandable, if contemptible—among those whose forefathers were perpetrators of the genocide. Such denial have at least two motives: first, protection of the moral reputations of those people and that country responsible for the genocidal activity (which seems the primary motive for those scholars and politicians who deny that massive genocide campaigns were carried out against American Indians); and second, on occasion, the desire to continue carrying out virulent racist assaults upon those who were the victims of the genocide in question (as seems to be the major purpose of the anti-Semitic so-called historical revisionists who claim that the Jewish Holocaust never happened or that its magnitude has been exaggerated).[13]

---

[12] Charney, 20.
[13] Stannard, 152.

Group Experience

The third characteristic that will be addressed is that of the group experience. Human beings need to be together and interact with each other. The need for companionship is strong for both physical as well as emotional fulfillment. Keeping in mind the fact that because a group is composed of many different individuals the potential for evil in the group is ever present. Hence the saying that every group has its "ten percent." Activities of a group can often be irresistible, enticing members to be caught up in the frenzy of uncontrolled immoderate indulgence. In this hypnotic state individuals are judgmentally challenged and are vulnerable to participating in actions through the acceptance of values that would not be acceptable to them under normal circumstances.[14]

Many times humans find themselves in group situations that start out harmless enough but, despite the best restraint of the individuals, the group dynamic feeds itself until the situation escalates out of control. For example, visualize the scene of a main street in a college town following a homecoming game upset. The street fills with crowds of unhappy fans intermingled with the jubilant fans of the winning team. Taunting words of banter are exchanged causing tempers to flare. Eventually one person pushes another, then fists are thrown, and others begin to join the fight. It does not take long before the streets turn into an uncontrollable melee. People, who normally would not prescribe to violence and destruction of property, soon find themselves as active participants. It may be from the fear of not being part of the group or simply because the group is conducting itself in this manner that makes the action perceived as acceptable.

---

[14] Charney, 114.

Even if one has not actively participated in this type of phenomenon we have all fallen prey to passing thoughts of violence in our minds. Most of us have learned of historical conquerors that led armies to the destruction of entire societies or cultures. Most Americans were witnesses to the violence incited, in Los Angeles, by the Rodney King trial of 1992.

The group transmits its experiences contagiously throughout its individual make up while forming a unique identity and history. This process slowly develops a type of subculture within the group. The group atmosphere provides comfort to those who fear loneliness and can become the way for people to avoid being an individual, thus surrendering their identity to the group. Often people become so involved in the group that their commitment blinds them to reality. Israel Charney explains:

> In the intoxication of group experiences, many people virtually surrender their entire individuality to the group and practically blend themselves into the group identity. They are now no longer themselves, and, therefore, they are more available to conformity to any instructions they are given just because those instructions come from a leader. Caught up in mass group frenzy, those people are no longer responsible for their decisions or choices (although I again emphasize that nothing of this effort to understand is intended to excuse the responsibility for one's choices). In a deep psychological sense, such people are no longer individuals. … The dynamic of needing to be committed to one's group ideology, whatever it is, is frequently a more powerful force than allegiance to the actual ideology. Thus, some good people who originally intended sincerely to support decent human values of liberation or freedom end up, almost without knowing it, staying with their group when it turns to guillotining, torturing, oppressing, and destroying—all in the name of liberty or freedom. No matter that the group process is moving toward destructiveness, those people are so mesmerized and paralyzed by their dependency on the group for purpose and continuity in their lives that they fail to notice or to be able to stand up to take action against the very destructiveness they once sincerely opposed.[15]

Role of Leaders

---

[15] Charney, 118-119.

Leadership is an awesome responsibility as it bears the burden of the actions of the group. In almost any great accomplishment or atrocity the recognition for success or failure is awarded to the leader. Leaders are seen as the source of ideas, motivation, rationalization or legitimation. Keep in mind that leaders are individuals and are susceptible to the aspects mentioned previously in the individual experience. As the success of the group expands they also become enthralled in the group experience. That in mind, power can be a strong motivator in the mind of a leader. The potential for evil is dependent on the personality, thought process, and education of the leader. Many articulate, respected people in positions of authority can easily rationalize, justify or legitimate violence against other people under the guise of a better society and, since people in groups tend to be sheep-like, they will follow their leaders orders to the fullest. The leader has gained the permission of society thus, making the violence acceptable. If the leaders' authority goes unchecked, it can readily lead to destructiveness. Israel Charney illustrates the possibilities within the United States:

> Some observers see various forces in the culture process in the United States that line up for and against the possibilities of a U.S.—made genocide. On one hand, there is the enormous vitality of the system of checks and balances within the structure of the U.S. government, and there is an electoral process that is largely responsible to the collective power of the people. The history of the United States shows that the people are capable of stopping massacres and are capable of bringing about the removal of leaders from office. On the other hand, in many ways the U.S. tradition continues to be frontierlike and therefore tends to accept power and violence as everyday facts of life. Everyday violence continues to dominate much of the life in the United States, amid the grandeur of plenty and creativity. The U.S. tradition is also overwhelmingly committed to the values of pragmatism or efficiency, which often compete against the people's needs and humanistic values. … The United States is given to a self-righteousness that gives rise to a seductive rationalization of violent power. These various trends in the collective U.S. experience make possible periodic genocidal campaigns against other people: the war in Vietnam (seen as a whole or in events such as My Lai); some would say the use of the atomic bomb; the campaign against the

Philippines earlier in this century; and certainly, the early—and, strangely, still-celebrated—history of the white man's subjugation of the Indians.[16]

TWENTIETH CENTURY

The destructiveness of genocide is not new to history. It has, however, become a crime of the recent era due to several factors: globally nationalism has intensified, scientific theories have been misused to promote beliefs about racial or ethnic superiority, and the information media has become widespread.[17] Dr. Raphael Lemkin elevated the serious issue of genocide to the international level with his coining and defining the term in his book, *Axis Rule in Occupied Europe*, published in 1944. After constant pressure from lobbyists, the United Nations took action, in 1946, unanimously adopting the following resolution:

> Genocide is a denial of the right of existence of entire human groups, as homicide is the denial of the right to live of individual human beings; such denial of the right of existence shocks the conscience of mankind, results in great losses to humanity in the form of cultural and other contributions represented by these human groups, and is contrary to moral law and to the spirit and aims of the United Nations.
> Many instances of such crimes of genocide have occurred when racial, religious, political and other groups have been destroyed, entirely or in part.
> The punishment of the crime of genocide is a matter of international concern.[18]

It took an additional two years of dispute over phraseology before, in 1948, the United Nations adopted the Convention on the Prevention and Punishment of the Crime of Genocide:

TEXT OF THE CONVENTION

---

[16] Charney, 197.
[17] Grolier.com the New Book of Knowledge Encyclopedia, accessed 14 Dec 2001
[18] Yearbook of the United Nations 1946-47, 255.

The Contracting Parties,

Having considered the declaration made by the General Assembly of the United Nations in its resolution 96 (I) dated 11 December 1946 that genocide is a crime under international law, contrary to the spirit and aims of the United Nations and condemned by the civilized world;

Recognizing that all periods of history genocide has inflicted great losses on humanity; and

Being convicted that, in order to liberate mankind from such an odious scourge, international co-operation is required:

Hereby agree as hereinafter provided:

ARTICLE I

The Contracting Parties confirm that genocide, whether committed in time of peace or in time of war, is a crime under international law which they undertake to prevent and to punish.

ARTICLE II

In the present Convention, genocide means any of the following acts committed with intent to destroy, in whole or in part, a national, ethnical, racial, or religious group, as such:

(a) Killing members of the group;
(b) Causing serious bodily or mental harm to the members of the group;
(c) Deliberately inflicting on the group conditions of life calculated to bring about its physical destruction in whole or in part;
(d) Imposing measures intended to prevent births within the group;
(e) Forcibly transferring children of the group to another group.

ARTICLE III

The following acts shall be punishable:

(a) Genocide;
(b) Conspiracy to commit genocide;
(c) Direct and public incitement to commit genocide;
(d) Attempt to commit genocide
(e) Complicity in genocide.

ARTICLE IV

Persons committing genocide or any of the acts enumerated in article III shall be punished, whether they are constitutionally responsible rulers, political officials, or private individuals.[19]

Forty-three countries signed the Convention on the Prevention and Punishment of the Crime of Genocide by the end of December 1949. Twenty ratifications were required for the convention to come into force, which it did in 1951.[20] Nations ratifying the convention agreed that international intervention was permitted even if a government, within its own territory, committed the genocidal acts. Although the United States signed the convention in 1948, they refused to ratify it for many years. The U.S. Senate was reluctant to subject American citizens to the jurisdiction of any world court. The United States finally ratified the convention in 1986.[21]

David Stannard points out that since the Genocide Convention was ratified many contend that the Convention's definition is too confined because it excludes political groups as potential victims or too expansive because physical or psychological affects are often applicable to situations that are not considered genocide. The fact remains that the Convention's definition remains the most widely accepted definition of genocide throughout the world.[22]

Being now armed with the definition and understanding of genocide and several of its characteristics turn towards the early history of the United States to evaluate the treatment of the Cherokee Indian. The following chapters will illustrate the struggle of the Cherokee Indian and the United States to coexist. The chronological sequence of significant events, occasional atrocities, and significant people will tell the plight of two

---

[19] Yearbook of the United Nations 1948-49, 959.
[20] Yearbook of the United Nations 1948-49, 961-962.
[21] Grolier.com Grolier Multimedia Encyclopedia, accessed 14 Dec 2001.
[22] Stannard, 280-281.

nations in their early attempts to coexist. Throughout the text will be sometimes undisguised and sometimes subtle incidents of will projection. As the following pages are consumed take time to digest the information and then reflect on the previous chapter before deciding if the name of the atrocity committed is genocide.

ERA OF PROMISE

(1785 – 1819)

Troubled times and periods of strife where nothing new to the Cherokee Indian by the latter part of the eighteenth century. For years they had allied with the British first against the French and later against the Colonists who would soon become known as Americans. Throughout these years they had suffered a serious impact to their survival as an Indian Nation. The Cherokee had suffered through the destruction of their homes and crops, by fire, while many of them where chased into the wilderness or even killed. It wasn't long before the Cherokee and their culture were near extinction.

Following the War for Independence the Cherokee began a struggle to reconstitute their losses. In this endeavor they would face the United States as it developed its sovereignty. To better understand the benchmark from where the Cherokee initial position was in 1785 one should look to the ideology of the founding fathers. As General George Washington fought several Indian tribes during the course of the Revolutionary War he had developed a dislike for them and thought of them as some thing less than human. David Stannard explains Washington's view as, "The Indians, this writer said, 'were hunted like wild beasts' in a 'war of extermination,' something Washington approved of since, as he was to say in 1783, the Indians, after all, were little different from wolves, 'both being beasts of prey, tho' they differ in shape.'"[23] He further believed that the object of federal policy should be to displace the Indian population west of the Mississippi. Thus in 1782 future President George Washington was searching for a way to pay troops who fought in the Revolutionary War. Ward Churchill explains that the costs associated with the seizure of native territory were avoided by convincing the Indians to cede the lands desired by the United States in exchange for a promise of protection of their remaining territory.

Federal troops were then paid with land grants generated from the prior Indian lands. This accomplished the United States government then could systematically remove the Cherokee, voluntarily or by force, west to lands yet to be claimed by the United States.[24] According to Alan Axelrod, "George Washington imagined a western 'Chinese wall' to separate whites and Indians."[25] This view is not to place Washington in a discreditable light, but rather it suggests the generally accepted methods, established by European conquests, of dealing with indigenous peoples.

One might say that the policy initially established to deal with the Indians was shortsided in that it did not account for the tremendous growth that the United States would realize in the coming years. Duane King adds that the Cherokee Indian most likely suffered more than any other Indian by ceding their land under the provisions of numerous treaties following the Revolutionary War. The demand for land fueled by the concept of Manifest Destiny and the inability of the Indians to provide unified resistances were the main factors in the evolution of the treaties.[26]

That background provided it is further important to understand the political mind of the Cherokee Indian. Cherokee political organization was based on traditional ideals intermingled with the civilized elements of the white man. One differing aspect was that the Cherokee recognized no higher authority than the town. A town council would gather to make decisions regarding nearly all aspects that impacted the town.[27] Due to the nature of the Cherokee Indian conflict among members was to be avoided. As Duane King has noted:

> If, after maneuvering, the sentiments of any one group could not be accommodated, it was expected to withdraw to avoid open conflict. In such cases, groups which withdrew were not bound by the decision reached.

---

[23] Stannard, 119.

[24] Ward Churchill, *A Little Matter Of Genocide: Holocaust and Denial in the Americas, 1492 to the Present* (San Francisco: City Lights Books, 1997), 210.

[25] Alan Axelrod, *Chronicle of the Indian Wars Colonial Times to Wounded Knee* (New York: Prentice Hall General Reference, 1993), 137.

[26] Richard W. Iobst, *The Cherokee Indian Nation: A Troubled History*. Ed. Duane H. King. (Knoxville: The Tennessee University Press, 1979), 181-182.

[27] King, 93.

19

The need for unanimity in councils and the lack of coercive power by the leaders were reflections of a central theme in Cherokee culture. Harmony and the avoidance of open conflict were highly valued in interpersonal relationships. A good man was one who did not create discord. Instead, he was cautious with his dealings with others, taking care not to be too forward with his own interests. If a conflict became unavoidable, he was expected to withdraw both emotionally, and, if possible, physically. The desire to create and maintain harmony was a strong and guiding principle in Cherokee politics.[28]

Though this mind set may be an honorable one it would prove to put the Cherokee at an immense disadvantage and most likely was a facilitator of the demise of their sovereignty.

The Treaty of Hopewell, November 28, 1975, was the first treaty between the United States and the Cherokee Nation. "The United States," writes Francis Prucha, " signed treaties with the southern tribes at Hopewell, South Carolina, in 1785 and 1786. These treaties fixed boundaries for the Indian country, withdrew protection from white settlers on Indian lands, made arrangements for the punishment of criminals, and provided trade regulations."[29] The Treaty of Hopewell guaranteed the Cherokee the protection of the United States government and no other sovereign whosoever and vows them security from oppression.

The Northwest Ordinance was passed on July 13, 1787. Francis Prucha comments that, "This legislation which established the Northwest Territory, thus inaugurating the policy of organizing and governing the national domain west of the Appalachians, included a firm statement of good faith and justice in dealing with the Indians."[30] The legislation promised the Indians that their land would never be taken from them without their consent and that they would not be invaded unless justly authorized by Congress. This legislation was an effort to preserve peace and harmony between the United States and the Indian Nations.

As the time passed the Cherokee began to adopt certain aspects of civilized life. This was a realized necessity if they were to survive economically with the white man. During the transition process they turned to the advice of George Washington for assistance. According to

---

[28] King, 94.

[29] Francis Paul Prucha, *Documents of United States Indian Policy* 3rd ed. (Lincoln and London: University of Nebraska Press, 2000), 6.

[30] Prucha, 9.

Duane King, President Washington, understanding the productive potential of the Cherokee land, encouraged them to cultivate corn, wheat, cotton, and flax. Doing this would produce food for Cherokee use as well as provide income through sales to whites. He further recommended that Cherokee women spin and weave. Going a step further President Washington directed the government agent to provide the tools and instruction to the Cherokee to facilitate the process.[31] Life and survival for the Cherokee was promising as they began to gain the material evidence of a civilized people. Due to their initial success, they found that their traditional method of communal property ownership would not suffice. As each man prospered there needed to be a manner in which he could protect the fruits of his efforts. The result was the consolidation and centralization of political power within the Cherokee government.[32] Further signs of civilization during this time period are slave holding, trading, and intermarriage. With intermarriage came the acceptance of mixed-blood individuals in the Indian society. The first school in Indian lands was also established in 1801 and eventually in 1808 the Cherokee formally adopted a legal code.

In 1801 Thomas Jefferson was elected President. His views were similar to those of Washington's when it came to Indian policy. In 1803 the ideology of Manifest Destiny intensified with the Louisiana Purchase. With this purchase came the thought that the United States would evolve into a continental nation. This would place the Indian in a "vise' with civilized populations approaching him from both sides and no where for him to be moved to avoid being an obstacle to progression.[33] As David Stannard has noted, in 1807 President Jefferson:

> Instructed his Secretary of War that any Indians who resisted American expansion into their lands must me met with "the hatchet." "And … if ever we are constrained to lift the hatchet against any tribe," he wrote, "we will never lay it down till that tribe is exterminated, or is driven beyond the Mississippi," continuing: "in war, they will kill some of us; we shall destroy all of them." These were not offhand remarks, for five years later, in 1812, Jefferson again concluded that white Americans were "obliged" to drive the "backward" Indians "with the beasts of the forests into the Stony Mountains"; and

---

[31] King, 113.
[32] King, 114.
[33] Chruchill, 219.

one year later still, he added that the American government had no other choice before it than "to pursue [the Indians] to extermination, or drive them to new seats beyond our reach."… Had these same words been enunciated by a German leader in 1939, and directed at European Jews, they would be engraved in modern memory. Since they were uttered by one of America's founding fathers, however, the most widely admired of the South's slaveholding philosophers of freedom, they conveniently have become lost to most historians in their insistent celebration of Jefferson's wisdom and humanity.[34]

Unfortunately for the Cherokee, during this time another formative figure and future President of the United States also shared this grim view of the Cherokee Indian. John Ehle points out that Andrew Jackson was, "convinced that Indians would not become civilized. He cherished all of his convictions, but most of all that one. The Cherokees were a roadblock in the way, isolating Tennessee. They made it blisteringly difficult for Tennessee to join the Union in any respect more than name."[35]

Despite General Jackson's perception of the Cherokee he enlisted their assistance during the War of 1812. The significance of this war for the Indians, was the fact that they would lose their option of allying with a nation other than the United States. This war against Great Britain also involved the Creek Indians in a Civil War. Their Nation was divided into a pro-American faction (the White Sticks) and a pro-British faction (the Red Sticks). The Cherokee fielded nineteen companies of warriors to ally with Jackson against the Red Sticks. During this campaign against the Red Sticks, General Jackson gained notoriety for his victory at the Battle of Horseshoe Bend in March 1814. It was following this victory, claims Ward Churchill, that his dehumanizing attitude shone as he allowed men under his charge to mutilate "800 or more Creek Indian corpses—the bodies of men, women and children that they had massacred—cutting off their noses to count and preserve a record of the dead, slicing long strips of flesh from their bodies to tan and turn into bridle reins."[36] This point is made not to villianize then Major General Andrew Jackson, but to point out the fact that this activity was sanctioned by an influential leader

---

[34] Stannard, 120.
[35] John Ehle, *Trail of Tears: The Rise And Fall Of The Cherokee Nation* (New York: Doubleday, a division of Bantam Doubleday Dell Publishing Group, Inc., 1988), 107.
[36] Churchill, 186.

22

of men and thus allowed the perception of acceptability to boundlessly transcend this event possibly influencing generations to follow.

For their efforts during the War of 1812 the Cherokees were also mistreated. Upon their return home they found that the Tennessee Militia had preceded them. The Tennesseans, "Had stolen horses, torn down fences, taken corn and maple sugar, and terrified the old people and the children."[37] The Cherokee were not remunerated in any fashion for what they had lost as a result of this pillaging. It was not a year later that the Cherokee Indian would again be slighted by Jackson's recommendation. The victory against the British at the Battle of New Orleans saw the Cherokee Indians as a rightful benefactor of a portion of the gained in the Mississippi Valley. The land had been in use by the Cherokee for many years and according to John Ehle, "Jackson knew full well that the Cherokees had equal claim to this area of three thousand square miles, but he wanted the land. The Cherokees had done well in the war, he admitted. Now let them be helpful in times of peace."[38]

During the period of James Madison's Presidency the Cherokee saw a glimpse of hope in the newly founded American Board of Commissioners for Foreign Missions that believed:

> The board favored Indian rights and opposed slavery, and it had developed wide political influence. On the board sat business and political leaders, including Congressmen, and financing of its missions all over the world came from wealthy merchants and industrialists, church members and pastors, most of them Congressionalists and Presbyterians. They saw the board as a chance to mold the evolving new United States, to influence it along New England lines, and to help slow down its growth and make government action more humane. Believing God had ordained them, as well as America, for great achievement, the board set out to educate and politically to influence the Indians of the South, and they saw at once that the tribe best able to advance was the Cherokee.[39]

Running counter to this light of promise was increased pressure from land hungry farmers, plantation owners, governors, and congressmen. To appease this desire for progress President Madison agreed that Indians would be best advised to move westward voluntarily.

---

[37] Ehle, 121.
[38] Ehle, 123.
[39] Ehle, 124-125.

The Cherokee continued to grow during this period through the assistance of the missionaries' schools and churches were established to provide educational opportunities. The General Crimes Act came into effect in 1817 which was the first law that provided for federal jurisdiction over the Indians on their own lands. Additionally the Cherokee saw the U.S. mail service provided throughout their lands. Also to come was the Exchange Treaty, which established eastern lands for the Cherokee and equal parcels in present day Arkansas.[40] A number of Cherokee Indians, realizing their eventual fate took advantage of this treaty moved west. Russell Thornton asserts that, "Records indicate that though 2,190 Cherokees enrolled to remove to the West from 1817 to 1819, after the treaty of 1817, only 1,102 actually went."[41]

Throughout the years of the Era of Promise the Cherokee Indian had altered his "savage" ways and adapted to the ways of the white man. Many Cherokee Indians had prospered well, educating their population and striving for self-government. In many regions intermarriage and mixed blood populations had even become acceptable. Despite the hardship and setbacks they had suffered along the way it appeared that they might be able to coexist as a nation within the boundaries of the United States. Soon this brief period of optimism would be put to the test and eventually crumble, as the ideology of Manifest Destiny would propel the United States to a continental nation.

---

[40] Wilma Mankiller and Michael Wallis, *Mankiller: A Chief and Her People* (Knoxville: University of Tennessee Press, 1979), 264.
[41] Russell Thorton, *The Cherokees: A Population History* (Lincoln and London: University of Nebraska Press, 1992), 49.

PERIOD OF DISSENSION

(1820 – 1838)

A census taken in 1820 recorded the Cherokee population at approximately 17,000. The census indicated that approximately 11,000 of them resided east of the Mississippi.[42] Though the Cherokee were beginning to flourish, 1820 brought the rumblings of the United States Indian removal policy. As negotiations over land cessions continued, one missionary wrote the American Board of Commissioners for Foreign Missions stating a removal of the Cherokee would adversely impact, if not ruin, the ultimate desire of assimilating or civilizing the Cherokee Indian. In spite of the Board's opinion they remained opposed to inference with state authority to govern.[43] Regardless of the opinions of others the Cherokee pressed forward with their struggle. In 1821 an Indian named Sequoyah (George Gist or Guess), had assembled an eighty five-character list or catalogue of the Cherokee language. This list spread rapidly throughout the Cherokee Nation in the east and in the west facilitating Cherokee literacy. During this time there was tension growing within the Cherokee Nation as the Old Settlers who had moved west were beginning the process of assimilation. John Ross the Chief of mainstream Cherokee in the east desired to create a single government for the entire Cherokee Nation.[44]

In 1824 the Secretary of War created the Bureau of Indian Affairs in the U.S. War Department. Since 1783 the Committee of Indian Affairs had handled Indian affairs. The War Department was created in 1789. Thus the renaming and movement of Indian Affairs into the War Department was indicative of things to come. The purpose of the new Bureau of Indian Affairs was to, record treaties and commitments made with the Indians, oversee all government interaction with Indian agencies, coordinate all liaison of Indian visits to Washington, D.C., and

---

[42] Thornton, 48.
[43] Ehle, 150.
[44] King, 151.

provide recommendations with respect to claims rising from laws and regulations governing the Indian Territories.

President Monroe, under pressure from the state of Georgia to extinguish Indian land titles within the state, proposed a voluntary removal policy as a best solution for the "Indian problem." The State of Georgia believed that they had been promised the removal of Indians from, within their borders, when they gave up their claim to lands in the west, as part of the Georgia Compact of 1802. Francis Prucha reports that President James Monroe provided the following message to the Senate and the House of Representatives on January 27, 1825:

> Being deeply impressed with the opinion that the removal of the Indian tribe from the lands which they now occupy within the limits of the several States and Territories to the country lying westward and northward thereof, within our acknowledged boundaries, is of very high importance to our Union, and may be accomplished on conditions and in a manner to promote the interest and happiness of those tribes, the attention of the Government has been long drawn with great solicitude to the object. … From the view I have taken of the subject I am satisfied that in the discharge of these important duties in regard to both the parties alluded to the United States will have to encounter no conflicting interests with either. On the contrary, that the removal of the tribes from the territory which they now inhabit to that which was designated in the message at the commencement of the session, which would accomplish the object for Georgia, under a well-digested plan for their government and civilization, which should be agreeable to themselves, would not only shield them from impending ruin, but promote their welfare and happiness. Experience has clearly demonstrated that in their present state it is impossible to incorporate them in such masses, in any form whatever, into our system. It has also demonstrated with equal certainty that without a timely anticipation of and provision against the dangers to which they are exposed, under causes which it will be difficult, if not impossible, to control, their degradation and extermination will be inevitable.[45]

The pressure to cede their lands continued to be unrelenting during these years. John Ehle emphasizes that despite Tennessean desire for Cherokee territory they considered the Cherokee not unlike their own kind. Georgians, on the other hand, had never grown to know the Cherokee and continuously fought with them. The Georgian mindset was that the states had joined to form the Union, thus they should retain the right not to be governed by the federal government. Georgians contend this in order that they might enact harsh laws at the state level to

---

[45] Prucha, 39.

make remaining in Georgia seem untenable for the Cherokee. They further believed that if Andrew Jackson were to become President of the United States, the federal government would become an ally vice a hindrance to their quest.[46]

The political organization of the Cherokee was undergoing continuous change due to pressure from dealings with the United States Government. The trend continued towards greater centralization ultimately resulting in the adoption of the Cherokee Constitution in 1828.[47] As further evidence of Cherokee social organization the publication of the *Cherokee Phoenix,* a bilingual and national newspaper, was printed. The combination of the publishing of the newspaper, the discovery of gold within the Indian lands, the election of Andrew Jackson as President, and the state of Georgia making Cherokee lands counties of the state, suggests Duane King, thrust the subject of removal to the forefront of debate.[48]

The policy of removing eastern Indians to the west of the Mississippi was met with ardent opposition from the Cherokees who believe they had a right to remain where they were. The Cherokee presented their argument with a great deal of sophistication and conviction. John Ehle provides the view of the Cherokee:

> If the agents of the United States purchase land for public object, such a purchase is not a treaty. If the State of Virginia, on the application of the United States, cedes a piece of land for a navy yard, or a fort, a compact of this sort is not a treaty. If the State of Georgia cedes to the United States all its claim to territory enough for two large new States, and the United States agree to make a compensation therefor, such cession and agreement are not a treaty. Accordingly, such negotiations are carried on and completed by virtue of laws of the National and State legislatures. Of course, compacts of this kind are never called treaties; and the idea of sending them to the Senate of the United States for ratification would be preposterous. One of the confederated States is not an independent community; nor can it make a treaty, either with the nation at large, or with any foreign power. But the Indian tribes and nations have made treaties with the United States during the last forty years, till the whole number of treaties thus made far exceeds a hundred, every one of which was ratified by the Senate before it became obligatory. Every instance of this kind implies that the Indian communities had governments of their own; that the Indians, thus living in communities, were not subject to the laws of the United States; and that they had rights and interests distinct from the rights and interests

---

[46] Ehle, 134.
[47] King, 93.
[48] King, 129.

of the people of the United States, and, in the fullest sense, public and national. All this is in accordance with facts; and the whole is implied in the single word *treaty*. ...

It is now contended by the politicians of Georgia, that the United States had no power to make treaties with Indians 'living,' as they express it '*within the limits of a sovereign and independent State*.' Thus, according to the present doctrine, General Washington and his advisors made a solemn compact, which they called a *treaty*, with certain Indians, whom they called *the Cherokee Nation*. In this compact, the United States bound the Cherokees not to treat with Georgia. Forty years have elapsed without any complaint on the part of Georgia, in regard to this exercise of the treaty-making power; but it is now found that the Cherokees are tenants at will of Georgia; that Georgia is the only community on earth that could treat with the Cherokees; and that they must now be delivered over to her discretion. The United States then, at the very commencement of our federal government, bound the Cherokees hand and foot, and have held them bound nearly forty years, and have thus prevented their making terms with Georgia, which might doubtless have been easily done at the time of the treaty of Holston. Now it is discovered, forsooth, that the United States *had no power to bind them at all.*[49]

According to Francis Prucha, Andrew Jackson's position was that the Cherokee had been allowed to exist in their lands only out of permission from the federal government rather than by right. Furthermore, it did not preclude the state government from exercising their own authority over their boundaries.[50] Following the debate, Congress passed the Indian Removal Act, authorizing President Jackson to exchange lands in the west for Indian lands in any state or territory. This initiated a forced relocation, beginning with the Southern tribes, to lands west of the Mississippi in order to prevent altercations with white settlers. Section five of the act guaranteed the Indians aid and assistance in removing and settling in to their new land as well as subsistence and support for their first year after their removal. While the United States government was struggling to organize the removal, dissention arose within the Cherokee government. As Duane King reports, Elias Boudinot, the editor of the *Cherokee Phoenix*, resigned due to a difference of opinion with John Ross. Boudinot believed that removal would be inevitable and thought that the paper should report both sides. John Ross desired to unite the

---

[49] Ehle, 228.
[50] Prucha, 45.

Cherokee against removal and only wanted his views printed in the *Cherokee Phoenix*. Following his resignation Boudinot eventually became the leader of the proremoval faction.[51]

In 1832 the Cherokee found another brief glimpse of hope when Mr. Chief Justice John Marshall of the United States Supreme Court ruled in favor of their rights. The case, Worcester vs. Georgia, was brought to the Supreme Court as a result of the imprisonment of Samuel A. Worcester. He was a missionary who refused to obey Georgia law that forbid whites to live in Cherokee country without pledging allegiance to the state and obtaining a permit. The decision maintained that the Cherokee were a distinct and independent nation free from the jurisdiction of the state. Chief Justice Marshall's opinion was noted in the Worcester v. Georgia decision:

> The very term "nation" so generally applied to them, means "a people distinct from others." The Constitution, by declaring treaties already made, as well as those to be made, to be the supreme law of the land, has adopted and sanctioned the previous treaties with the Indian nations, and consequently admits their rank among those powers who are capable of making treaties. The words "treaty" and "nation" are words of our own language, selected in our diplomatic and legislative proceedings, by ourselves, having each a definite and well understood meaning. We have applied them to Indians, as we have applied them to the other nations of the earth. They are applied to all in the same sense.[52]

It soon became evident that President Jackson would not enforce the decision of the Supreme Court. John Ridge, a Cherokee, who had allied with Andrew Jackson during the War of 1812, visited the President at the White House to inquire what Andrew Jackson intended to do about the situation. The President conveyed to John Ridge that the only hope for the Cherokee was to give up their land in Georgia and voluntarily remove to the west. As John Ehle reports, "The lanky President with the deeply lined face was not going to bother with broken pieces and bits; the momentum of his administration was established."[53]

Over the next few years, despite the efforts of Chief Ross to maintain unity in the face of aggression, the Cherokee nation fractured once more with the advent of the Treaty party. Duane

---

[51] King, 139.
[52] Prucha, 60.
[53] Ehle, 255.

King adds, that the Treaty party realized that living in the areas claimed by Georgia would lead to the extinction of their way of life and promoted the cession of their lands as a means of salvation. Their discord facilitated the separation of the Cherokee nation further.[54]

John Ehle provides further sentiment of President Jackson in a letter signed by Jackson that was printed in newspapers on April 7, 1835. An excerpt from the letter read as:

> You are now place in the midst of a white population. Your peculiar, customs which, regulated your intercourse with one another, have been abrogated by the great political community among which you live; and you are now subject to the same laws which now govern the other citizens of Georgia and Alabama. You are liable to prosecutions for offenses, and to civil nations for a breach of any of your contracts. Most of your young people are uneducated, and are liable to be brought into collision at all times with their white neighbors. Your young men are acquiring habits of intoxication. With strong passions, and without those habits of restraint which our laws inculcate and render necessary, they are frequently driven to excesses which must eventually terminate into their ruin. The game has disappeared among you and you must depend upon agriculture and the mechanical arts for support. And, yet, a large portion of your people have acquired little or no property in the soil itself, or in any article of personal property which can be useful to them. How, under these circumstances, can you live in the country you now occupy? Your condition must become worse and worse, and you will ultimately disappear, as so many tribes have done before you.
>   I have no motive, my friends, to deceive you. I am sincerely desirous to promote your welfare. Listen to me, therefore, while I tell you that you cannot remain where you now are. Circumstance that cannot be controlled, and which are beyond the reach of human laws, render it impossible that you can flourish in the midst of a civilized community. You have but one remedy within your reach. And that is, to remove to the West and join your countrymen, who are already established there. And the sooner you do this, the sooner you will commence your career of improvement and prosperity.[55]

With the guidance of President Jackson, Francis Prucha comments that, the United States government eventually capitalized on the Cherokee Indian's fractured leadership by negotiating with the Treaty Party leaders. Although the Treaty Party spoke for only a small fraction of the Cherokee Indian they agreed to the terms of and signed the Treaty of New Echota near the end of 1835.[56] By signing the Treaty of New Echota the Cherokee surrendered their title to all Cherokee lands in the Southeast in exchange for lands in the Indian Territory. Also during this year the Georgia State guard seized *the Cherokee Phoenix* press putting an end to the six-year publication.

---

[54] King, 149.
[55] Ehle, 275-276.
[56] King, 149.

Since only a fraction of the Cherokee nation subscribed to the Treaty of New Echota the majority believed that they would not be bound by the terms of the treaty.[57] This belief would soon begin to dissipate as Congress ratified the treaty in 1836.

General John Ellis Wool was sent to quell Indian aggressions, as a result of recent government actions. John Ehle adds, General Wool wrote the Secretary of War the following in the fall of 1836, "The duty I have to perform is far from pleasant. ... only made tolerable with the hope that I may stay cruelty and injustice, and assist the wretched and deluded beings called Cherokees, who are only the prey of the most profligate and most vicious of white men."[58]

Even Ralph Waldo Emerson would come to the defense of the Cherokee when he learned of the injustices being committed against them. He sent a letter to President Martin Van Buren commenting on the favorable value and strides in civilized progress of the Cherokee Indian. Emerson stated his contention and disbelief of the rumored government treatment of the Cherokee. John Ehle acknowledges that Emerson wrote on behalf of citizens from Maine to Georgia, "Such a dereliction of all faith and virtue, such a denial of justice, and such deafness to screams for mercy were never heard of in times of peace and in the dealings of a nation with its own allies and wards, since the earth was made."[59]

The pleas for reconsideration fell on deaf ears. The United States government assigned General Winfield Scott to carry out the round up, internment, and displacement of the Cherokee Indian. In May of 1838 He published his order to the Cherokee Indians:

> *Cherokees!* The President of the United States has sent me, with a powerful army, to cause you, in obedience to the Treaty of 1835, to join that part of your people who are already established in prosperity, on the other side of the Mississippi. Unhappily, the last two years which where allowed for the purpose, you have suffered to pass away without following, and without making any preparation to follow, and now, or by the time that this solemn *address* shall reach your distant settlements, the emigration must be commenced in haste, but, I hope, without disorder. I have no power, by granting a farther delay, to correct the error that you have committed. The full moon of Mat is

---

[57] King, 144.
[58] Ehle, 302.
[59] Ehle, 303.

already on the wane, and before another shall have passed away, every Cherokee man, women and child, in those States, must be in motion to join their brethren in the far West.

My Friends! This is no sudden determination on the part of the President, whom you and I must now obey. By the treaty, the emigration was to have been completed on, or before, the 23ʳᵈ of this month, and the President has constantly kept you warned, during the two years allowed, through all his officers and agents in this country, that the Treaty would be enforced.

I am come to carry out that determination. My troops already occupy many positions in this country that you are to abandon, and thousands, and thousands are approaching, from every quarter, to render resistance and escape alike hopeless. All those troops, regular and militia, are you friends. Receive them and confide in them as such. Obey them when they tell you that you can remain no longer in this country. Soldiers are as kind hearted as brave, and the desire of every one of us is to execute our painful duty in mercy. We are commanded by the President to act towards you in that spirit, and such is also the wish of the whole people of America.

Chiefs, head-men and warriors! Will you, then, by resistance, compel us to resort to arms? God forbid! Or will you, by flight, seek to hide yourselves in mountains and forests, and thus oblige us to hunt you down? Remember that, in pursuit, it may be impossible to avoid conflicts. The blood of the white man, or the blood of the red man, may be split, and if split, however accidentally, it may be impossible for the discreet and humane among you, or among us to prevent a general war and carnage. Think of this my Cherokee brethren! I am an old warrior, and have been present at many a scene of slaughter; but spare me, I beseech you, the horror of witnessing the destruction of the Cherokees.

Do not, I invite you, even wait for the close approach of the troops; but make such preparations for emigration as you can, and hasten to this place, the Ross' Landing, or to Gunter's Landing, where you all will be received in kindness by officers selected for the purpose. You will find food for all, and clothing for the destitute, at either of those places, and thence at your ease, and in comfort, be transported to your new homes according to the terms of the Treaty.

This is the address of a warrior to warriors. May his entreaties be kindly received, and may the God of both prosper the Americans and Cherokees, and preserve them long in peace and friendship with each other![60]

General Scott was involved in every detail of the displacement. His soldiers did not have his trust, as he was concerned about their attitude toward the Indians. The Tennesseans and North Carolinians typically were receptive to the Cherokee. The Georgians by contrast, in many cases vowed to not return home until they had killed at least one Indian. It is for this reason that General Scott remained personally with the Georgian division.[61]

The Cherokee Indians suffered tremendously under the abuse of weather and soldiers along the journey to the West. David Stannard explains that the Trail of Tears:

---

[60] Ehle, 324-325.
[61] Ehle, 328.

In fact, the "relocation" was nothing less than a death march—a Presidentially ordered death march that, in terms of the mortality rate directly attributable to it, was almost as destructive as the Bataan Death March of 1942, the most notorious Japanese atrocity in all of the Second World War. About 22,000 Cherokee then remained in existence, 4000 of whom had already broken under the pressures of white oppression and left for Indian Territory. Another thousand or so escaped and hid out in the Carolina hills. The remaining 17,000 were rounded up by the American military and herded into detention camps—holding pens, really—where they waited under wretched and ignominious conditions for months as preparations for their forced exile were completed. James Mooney, who interviewed people who had participated in the operation, described the scene: Under Scott's orders the troops were disposed at various points throughout the Cherokee country, where stockade forts were erected for gathering in and holding the Indians preparatory to removal. From these, squads of troops were sent to search out with rifle and bayonet every small cabin hidden away in the coves or by the sides of mountain streams, to seize and bring in as prisoner all the occupants, however or wherever they might be found. Families at dinner were startled by the sudden gleam of bayonets in their doorway and rose up to be driven with blows and oaths along the weary miles of trail that led to the stockade. Men were seized in their fields or going along the road, women were taken from their wheels and children from their play. In many cases, on turning for one last look as they crossed the ridge, they saw their homes in flames, fired by the lawless rabble that followed on the heels of the soldiers to loot and pillage. So keen were these outlaws on the scent that in some instances they were driving off the cattle and other stock of the Indians almost before the soldiers has fairly started their owners in the other direction. Systematic hunts were made by the same men for Indian graves, to rob them of their silver pendants and other valuables deposited with the dead. A Georgia volunteer, afterward a colonel in the confederate service, said: "I fought through civil war and have seen men shot to pieces and slaughtered by the thousands, but the Cherokee removal was the cruelest work I ever knew."

An initial plan to carry the Cherokee off by steamboat, in the hottest part of the summer, was called off when so many of them died from disease and the oppressive conditions. After waiting for the fall season to begin, they were driven overland, in groups upwards of about a thousand, across Tennessee, Kentucky, Illinois, and Missouri. One white traveler from Maine happened upon several detachments from the death march, all of them 'suffering extremely from fatigue of the journey, and the ill health consequent upon it": The last detachment which we passed on the 7th embraced rising two thousand Indians. … [W]e found the road literally filled with procession for about three miles in length. The sick and feeble were carried in wagons—about as comfortable for traveling as a New England ox cart with a covering over it—a great many ride on horseback and multitudes go on foot—even aged females, apparently nearly ready to drop into the grave, were traveling with heavy burdens attached to the back—on the sometimes frozen ground, and sometimes muddy streets, with no covering for the feet except what nature had given them. … We learned from the inhabitants on the road where the Indians passed, that they buried fourteen or fifteen at every stopping place, and they make a journey of ten miles per day only on an average. Like other governmental-sponsored Indian death marches this one intentionally took native men, women, and children through areas where it was known that cholera and other epidemic diseases were raging; the government sponsors of this march, again as with others, fed the Indians spoiled flour and rancid meat, and they drove the native people on through freezing rain and cold. Not a day passed without numerous deaths from the unbearable conditions under which they were forced to travel. And when they arrived in Indian Territory many more succumbed to fatal illness and starvation.[62]

Ward Chruchill confirms, "According to the most recent study, which is exceedingly thorough, about 55 percent of all Cherokees alive in 1838, when they were interned, died as a direct result of the extreme privations they suffered along the Trail."[63]

The removal to Indian Territory thrust the Cherokee back in time as they lost virtually everything they had amassed due to the nature of their departure and journey West. William Mcloughlin tells us that, since few Cherokee were actually able to transport their belongings to the west they were forced to revert to their ancient ways. For example, they fashioned bowls, pots, and dishes out of clay cooked over a fire while carving utensils out of wood. For years after their removal they used these instruments. Further they had to revert back to their "savage" means of hunting to obtain sustenance and clothing. All the progress made in their civilization had been taken from them as they were forced to survive in their new land.[64]

It is doubtful that the true extent of the damage done to the Cherokee will ever be completely realized. How does one tabulate the cost of a previously well adapted nation both politically and economically abandoning their way of life. Many Cherokees, asserts William Mcloughlin, departed from religion, turned to pursuits of gambling, drinking, and thievery. This fostered the perception of white explorers and settlers that the Cherokee did not have the motivation and self-control to thrive in a productive capacity.[65] One might suggest that these activities were in part due to the impact of displacement. Other unmeasurable and probably unintentional factors that Ward Churchill points out are, "the psychological effects on the Indians—acute anxiety, trauma, and oppression, generally referred as 'demoralization,' which … resulted from the kind of warfare…"[66] waged against them. The Cherokee Nation had suffered a

---

[62] Stannard, 123-124.
[63] Churchill, 144.
[64] William G. McLoughlin, *After the Trail Of Tears: The Cherokees' Struggle For Sovereignty 1839-1880* (Chapel Hill: The University of North Carolina Press, 1993), 35.
[65] McLoughlin, 39.
[66] Churchill, 150-151.

devastating blow. Although conditions seemed ruinous, the Cherokee would soon prove resilient in thought and action in pursuit of the prosperity of their Nation.

ENDEAVOR TOWARD SOVEREIGNTY

(1839 - 1907)

The United States government had seen its promise of removal through to fruition. Evidence suggests however that many of the promises associated with the removal proved to be hollow and less than accurate. William Mcloughlin illustrates the misrepresentation of the western lands:

> The Cherokee lands in the West included 5 million acres in northeastern Oklahoma in addition to the Neutral Lands and the Cherokee Outlet. While the federal government argued that it had given the Cherokees a valuable and fertile new homeland equivalent in size to its old homeland, the areas that were capable of growing corn or wheat and that provided both the water and timber necessary to building farms were not extensive. Much of the best land was already occupied by the Old Settlers. An agent of the federal government described the area (excluding the Cherokee Outlet) as containing "something less than 5,000,000 acres. Of this at least two-thirds are entirely unfit for cultivation. A large share of the tillable land is of an inferior quality. Most of the untillable land is entirely worthless, even for timber, as it consists of stony ridges and valleys covered with scrubby growth, mostly scrubby oak called black jack. There are few fine forests of very limited extent, also good timber of other kind on the streams and in the southern part of the nation. No country was ever less worthy of the high encomiums it has received" from those who justified the Cherokees' removal to it.[67]

Beyond the transgressions of land value, the United States government inadequately fulfilled their requirement to supply the Cherokee under the provisions of the treaty with the Old Settlers in 1828. Although the federal government provided the requisite number of spinning wheels, blacksmiths and wheelwrights the assistance was completely inadequate with respect to the number of Cherokee Indians ultimately displaced to the west.[68]

The period of dissention in the Cherokee nation created a divided nation. Three political parties had formed the Old Settlers, the Treaty party and the Ross party. The Old Settlers comprised those that had chosen to remove west early during the removal policy. The Treaty party comprised the small faction that signed the Treaty of New Echota. The Ross party included

---

[67] Mcloughlin, 35-37.
[68] Mcloughlin, 39.

the majority of the nation and where seen as the emigrants. Now that the nation had been removed west the Treaty party assimilated into the Old Settler government and the Old Settlers expected the emigrants to accept their government as well. The Old Settler government had been in place and functioning for ten years at this point. John Ross ardently opposed the unification of his people under laws and regulations that had been established before their arrival. Several conventions were held during 1839 in an attempt to unite the Cherokee nation with little results. Duane King observed that there was still a great deal dissatisfaction in the fractured nation that would facilitate continued disagreement and conflict from within. Additionally, the few Treaty Party members who agreed to the terms of the Treaty of New Echota were perceived as traitors and would most likely become victims of violent activity should they remain in the Cherokee nation.[69]

Throughout the next several years John Ross emerged as the dominant influence in the Cherokee nation and would continue to fight for national sovereignty in Washington, D.C. In 1840 John Ross was able to push forward the Act of Union which half-heartedly united the Cherokee nation. His efforts during this period were plagued by guerrilla warfare by those loyal to the Treaty party. Although these few enjoyed the rights and privileges of the Ross government they remained determined to disrupt the nation. Their actions continued to give the United States government the perception of an Indian uprising in the Cherokee nation so much as to cause the threat of U.S. Army intervention to maintain order in 1845.

Tom Starr, a key individual in the guerrilla warfare, developed a hatred of John Ross and vowed to prevent reconciliation between Treaty party and the Ross party. Any action taken by the Ross government to quell the violence found members of the Cherokee light horse patrol on the Starr gang execution list.[70] Duane King comments on this tumultuous time:

> The Cherokee nation reeled as it was buffeted by internal turbulence. Murders were common, armed bandits roamed the countryside, and hundreds of Cherokees (especially

---

[69] King, 154.
[70] Mcloughlin, 50.

Treaty party people) left the nation seeking refuge in Arkansas. Ross' police companies staged a liquidation campaign against the Starr family, of whom some were notorious outlaws, but others innocent of anything except identification with the Treaty party. A number of Treaty party men, armed and ready for battle, collected around Stan Watie, who lost a second brother, Thomas Watie, to Ross party's vengeance. Watie's force occupied Fort Wayne, an abandoned Arkansas army post on the border of the Indian Territory. Sporadic violence continued, and the threat of civil war hung over the Nation for more than one year.[71]

In 1846 President Polk suggested that since the Cherokee tribe could not exist in harmony it should be divided into two distinct tribes. Realizing that this was counter to all that he had been working towards, John Ross decided that a compromise must be reached in order to maintain unity and the sovereignty of the Cherokee nation. William Mcloughlin notes that the Treaty of 1846 brought peace to the Cherokee nation. Additionally, it ended the removal period since Ross finally accepted the terms of the Treaty of 1835. This event brought the funds promised by the United States government to offset removal losses by the Cherokee. This provided the Cherokee nation a needed boost towards economic recovery.[72]

The Cherokee began to prosper trading surplus corn, wheat, cotton, cattle, horses and hogs. Slavery was increased among the wealthier Cherokee. A testament to Cherokee prosperity was the development of three large towns within the nation. "Tahlequah," declares William Mcloughlin, "… contained the legislative buildings, the Supreme Court building, the Office of the *Cherokee Advocate*, a post office, eight stores, five hotels, three blacksmith shops, a tailor shop, a saddlery, a tannery, a shoemaker shop, a dentist, and several law offices, as well as residences of those who worked in the town"[73]

In 1849 the United States congress transferred the Office of Indian Affairs from the War Department to the newly created Department of the Interior. From this point to the onset of the American Civil War the Cherokee nation continued to grow and evolve. As it grew, a division developed between economic classes. The implication of William Mcloughlin is that Cherokee

---

[71] King, 157-158.
[72] Mcloughlin, 58.
[73] Mcloughlin, 81.

leadership contended that they were quite capable of self-government provided there was no outside federal or state government interference. A division eventually grew in the nation between the upper class who subscribed to the white American ways and the lower class who advocated a return to the traditional culture of Cherokee values. Peace was prevalent as long as the two groups refrained from interfering with one another. As the paths followed by the two groups was diametrically opposed civil strife soon erupted. By the mid-1800s the nation remained unified only to oppose American threats to their sovereignty.[74]

The peace and tranquility enjoyed during the years since 1846 was disrupted by the arousal of factional division among Cherokees. John Ross tried desperately to keep the Cherokee nation neutral, believing that the best interest of the survival of their nation depended upon maintaining positive relations with the United States government. Stand Watie, followed largely by former Treaty people, departed from his Ross's view and fielded a pro-slave regiment to aid the Confederate Army. Indicative of the division among the Cherokee nation was that the regiment under Stand Watie went to war with the Confederate Army not only for the slavery issue, but saw the grander ideology of ejecting the Ross government from power. Although Ross remained Unionist throughout the war he agreed to sign a treaty with the Confederate Army when the Union Forces abandoned the forts in the Indian Territory.[75]

In 1862 Union forces defeated Stand Watie's regiment at the Battle of Pea Ridge. Following this defeat Ross seized the opportunity to realign with the United States government. Union Forces invaded and occupied the Cherokee nation. The result was the American Civil War also divided the Cherokee nation. Duane King emphasizes:

> War in the Cherokee Nation became an intratribal conflict between the old factions, and it proved costly. The Cherokees' population was severely reduced (perhaps by 25 percent), the land was ravaged, and the Nation's polity was destroyed. Few people suffered more intensely during the Civil War than the Cherokees—four years of endemic

---

[74] Mcloughlin, 85.
[75] King, 160.

violence springing from factional animosity rather than from issues of war wasted the region and erased the constructive work of two decades.[76]

Peace in the Cherokee nation came to the Cherokee nation in June 1865 when Stand Watie finally surrendered. He was the last Confederate general to do so.[77]

Following the Civil War John Ross was reestablished as the leader of the Cherokee nation. Although the nation remained divided, the violent nature of the factionalism was history. The new looming threat to the Cherokee nation was the opening of the west. This evolution saw the railroads demanding right of way, frontiersmen desirous of rights to timber and minerals, and ranchers wishing to drive their cattle westward to railroad hubs.

Ward Chruchill explains the dominant posture taken by the United States government:

> At least as early as the administration of Ulysses S. Grant in the mid-1870s, there was an influential lobby which held that the final eradication of native cultures and population could be achieved more cost-effectively—and with a far greater appearance of "humanitarianism"—through a process of "assimilation" than by force of arms. ... the objective was to "kill the Indian, spare the man" ... in effect, it was the express goal of federal policy to bring about the "digestion" of what little remained of Native North America as rapidly and efficiently as possible.[78]

In 1887 the Dawes Act or General Allotment Act forced the termination of tribal held lands. This act attacked the bulwark of Indian culture, as their land was traditionally owned in common. This act suggested denationalization as the answer to "the Indian question." The Cherokee were initially exempt from the terms of the act, but this hope, as with the hope of previous negotiations with the United States government would not survive the test of time.

The final period of Cherokee sovereignty was a fruitless time during which leadership accepted the reality that their sovereignty would not last. In 1890, in the middle of Cherokee lands, the Oklahoma Territory was established. The Dawes Commission, in 1893, was authorized by Congress to negotiate with the Five Civilized Tribes for allotment of their lands. In 1898 the Curtis Act, accomplished what the Dawes Commission failed to, effectively abolish tribal

---

[76] King, 161.
[77] Mcloughlin, 219.
[78] Churchill, 245.

governments in Indian Territory. 1907 saw Oklahoma gain statehood. Following this the Cherokee were relegated to reservations and essentially were left a sovereignless people.

CONCLUSION

Genocide is a relatively new term that tends to be shrouded within the dark side of human nature. Was the United States government responsible for the pursuit of genocide of the Cherokee Indian? It must be stated forthrightly that the United States government never had an official policy of genocide against the Cherokee Indian. However, evidence has been provided that illustrates certain genocidal acts, as defined by the United Nations, were carried out against the Cherokee Indian as a result of governmental policy.

Article II of the Convention on the Prevention and Punishment of the Crime of Genocide outlines the criterion that substantiates genocide. Article II, item (a) Killing members of the group can be exemplified by the individual actions of Thomas Jefferson and Andrew Jackson acting in the role of leaders in this country's formative years. Although they may not have physically or officially ordained such activities, their well known and public verbalization of dehumanizing and exterminating the Indian, sanctified or legitimized this conduct towards the Cherokee in the minds of those they led.

The Removal Act of 1830 holds the elements that satisfy Article II, item (b) Causing serious bodily or mental harm to the members of the group. Although this Act was intended to make land exchanges for the voluntary displacement of the Cherokee, it ultimately was seen to fruition in a different fashion. Being forced from their homes, at times at the point of a bayonet and removed west with only what could be carried would obviously have a traumatic impact on any person subjected to that treatment. As a result of this process the Cherokee, in many instances, suffered devastating demoralization from which they would not recover.

The American Board of Commissioners for Foreign Missions voiced their opinion that removal would distress and retard the Cherokee population. This fact infers that those responsible for implementing the "policy of removal" knew beforehand that the methods employed during the removal policy would have, as its by product, the elements contained in

42

Article II, item (c) Deliberately inflicting on the group conditions of life calculated to bring about its physical destruction in whole or in part. Furthermore is that displacement found the Cherokee in an environment where he was not familiar with the climate. This would prove to make the first years of farming difficult as they did not know what crops were suitable nor when was the best time to plant. Coupled with the fact that the government failed to supply adequate materials to support a population the size of the Cherokee for their first year put the Cherokee at a serious disadvantage in terms of survival.

One might suggest that Article II, item (d) Imposing measures intended to prevent birth within the group could be met by the demoralizing effect of the Removal process. As Ward Churchill states:

> There is another subtext to the psychology of traumatic demoralization, much less remarked upon, although this too was never a great secret: in periods of severe stress and despair the ability of humans to procreate drops off dramatically. Under the conditions imposed upon American Indians, it could have been readily foreseen—and *was*—that their birthrates would plummet in rather direct correlation to their spiraling rates of death.[79]

The critical aspect of Article II is the word "intent." Is it conceivable that the fathers of this great nation intentionally committed acts in pursuit of this type of atrocity? Certainly that is not the case. Displacement of the Cherokee Indian was an inevitable progression, as the advanced EuroAmerican culture demanded a rapid change from the Cherokee for successful assimilation. The Cherokee were not able to adjust rapidly enough as a nation to meet the demands of ever increasing competition from developing EuroAmerican ideologies and demands for territory. Though the Cherokee may have been dealt with poorly, genocide is not the applicable term needed to describe this natural progression of civilized culture. This being the case, where does that leave us? What is the relevancy to the present day? What possible relevancy could there be to the military in today's climate?

---

[79] Churchill, 151.

Though genocide is not new to history, it has become a vogue term that is increasingly being used to describe actions against people or groups as crimes against humanity. The definition ratified by the United Nations continues to be contested to include an ever-expanding interpretation. The military, as ambassadors of our nation, must understand genocide and how to recognize it before becoming associated with its negative aspects. Recent experience has proven that the United States military has become increasingly more involved in conflicts of ethnic origin, involving civilians, worldwide. Over the past decade the term genocide has been associated with the conflict in Afghanistan, Bosnia, Iraq, Somalia, and Yugoslavia. The United States military has been actively involved in operations in all of these countries during this time. Even when the military is not directly involved, a Commander-In-Chief of the applicable region should be aware of the situation and its associated sensitivities.

No one doubts that the one who makes the rules is usually the one with the most economic resources and the largest military might. The United States as the one remaining super power has taken on many inherent responsibilities that accompany that status. One reason why genocide is relevant today is that many nations will form judgement of the United States based upon their traditional beliefs and previous actions. One of the strategic principles of war is "Know your Enemy, Yourself and Your Allies."[80] In today's environment the military leadership, specifically at the strategic level, must embrace the fact that part of knowing yourself is understanding how the United States is viewed by other nations. One might suggest that based on our past dealings with the American Indian our governmental policies have the perception of possibly being based on deceit. Many of recent military missions have been either humanitarian or peace keeping/enforcement. In order to maintain support, both external and internal to a country, military leadership must ensure that perceptions do not evolve into reality.

---

[80] Dr. Joe Strange, Perspectives on Warfighting Number Six Capital "W" War A Case for Strategic Principles of War (Quantico: the Marine Corps University contract via the Defense Automated Printing Service Center, 1998), 8.

Operation DESERT STORM was successful in removing the Iraqi Army from the borders of Kuwait in 1991. Overwhelming support of United States military action was clearly evident. However, the United States did not transition beyond that mission without accusations of genocidal activity. One clear illustration is the wording, used by military members during briefings, which described offensive actions as a "turkey shoot" or a "battle of annihilation." Are these words not unlike the phraseology used by Thomas Jefferson and Andrew Jackson to sanctify conduct towards the population of the foe? As David E. Stannard points out, General Norman Shwarzkopf inadvertently implicated himself, when making reference to the destruction of Romans at the hands of the Carthaginians in the third century B.C.:

> In his own words, that is what General Norman Shwarzkopf had hoped to create in Iraq. And when confronted by the press with evidence that appeared to demonstrate the American government's lack of concern for innocent civilians (including as many as 55,000 children) who died as a direct consequence of the war—and with a United States medical team's estimate that hundreds of thousands more Iraqi children were likely to die of disease and starvation caused by the bombing of civilian facilities—the Pentagon's response either was silence, evasion, or a curt "war is hell."[81]

In the aftermath of the Gulf War a War Crimes Commission of Inquiry was convened to examine whether combatants had violated International law.[82] Furthermore, United States policy since the end of the Gulf War has resulted in additional scrutiny as sanctions imposed upon Iraq continue to have diminishing results at the expense of the Iraqi populace. The policy of keeping a leader in check by slowly exterminating a population through sanctions begins to take on an appearance of genocide rather than national policy. William F. Donaher and Ross B DeBlois refer to this as "sanctions fatigue" in describing the loss of support for such policy.[83] Since the conduct of war, the military and the political objective are so closely interwoven the United States military forces need to be aware and conscious of genocide to avoid its negative impact on the

---

[81] Stannard, 254.

[82] *American Officials Charged For War Crimes*. http://www.thewinds.org/1997/02/war_crimes.html, accessed 01 March 2002.

[83] Donaher, William F. and Ross B. Deblois. "Is the Current UN and US Policy toward Iraq Effective?," Parameters: US Army War College Quarterly 31, no. 4 (Winter 2001-02): 112-125.

mission.

To further illustrate the point about perceptions consider William Blum's list of events he deems worthy of the term genocide or as he puts it, crimes against humanity:

> William Clinton, president, for his merciless bombing of the people of Yugoslavia for 78 days and nights, taking the lives of many hundreds of civilians, and producing one of the greatest ecological catastrophes in history; for his relentless continuation of the sanctions and rocket attacks upon the people of Iraq; and for his illegal and lethal bombings of Somalia, Bosnia, Sudan and Afghanistan.
>
> General Wesley Clark, Supreme Allied Commander in Europe, for his direction of the NATO bombing of Yugoslavia with an almost sadistic fanaticism..."He would rise out of his seat and slap the table. 'I've got to get the maximum violence out of this campaign-now!"
>
> George Bush, president, for the murder of hundreds of thousands of innocent Iraqi civilians, including many thousands of children, the result of his 40 days of bombing and the institution of draconian sanctions; and for his unconscionable bombing of Panama, producing widespread death, destruction and homelessness, for no discernible reason that would stand up in a court of law.
>
> General Colin Powell, Chairman of the Joint Chiefs of Staff, for his prominent role in the attacks on Panama and Iraq, the latter including destruction of nuclear reactors as well as plants making biological and chemical agents. It was the first time ever that live reactors had been bombed, and ran the risk of setting a dangerous precedent. Hardly more than a month had passed since the United Nations, under whose mandate the United States was supposedly operating in Iraq, had passed a resolution reaffirming its "prohibition of military attacks on nuclear facilities" in the Middle East. In the wake of the destruction, Powell gloated: "The two operating reactors they had are both gone, they're down, they're finished." He was just as cavalier about the lives of the people of Iraq. In response to a question concerning the number of Iraqis killed in the war, the good general replied: "It's really not a number I'm terribly interested in."
>
> And for his part in the cover up of war crimes in Vietnam by troops of the same brigade that carried out the My Lai massacre.
>
> General Norman Schwarzkopf, Commander in Chief, U.S. Central Command, for his military leadership of the Iraqi carnage; for continuing the carnage two days after the cease-fire; for continuing it against Iraqis trying to surrender.[84]

Although no one will ever be brought to trial for these unjustified accusations, the point is that in this era the United States and military leaders, as ambassadors of the Nation, must understand the political atmosphere when dealing with foreign nations prior to there being any interpretive hint of genocidal activity.

As recent as October 22, 2001 the Taliban has accused the United States of genocide, claiming the bombing of a hospital in Herat, Afghanistan. As the United States military executes National Policy in fighting terrorism, it must be on guard for situations of human nature that have the potential to escalate into genocidal activity. Just by briefly browsing the Internet in today's environment one can find several papers being circulated concerning civilian casualties and collateral damage that implicate the United States. The time is long past when collateral damage is acceptable in a military operation, particularly when associated with civilian casualties.

Finally, military leadership at all levels must maintain the capability to clearly articulate, to any potential audience, the purpose of the operation in which they are involved. The military has made great strides with rules of engagement education and should adopt a similar approach in educating its forces to deal with the media. For example, the development and dissemination of command messages and themes that apply to United States positions on current operations. By educating the force on these issues commanders can ensure that their forces will be able to confidently project the most favorable message to the media when the time arises. This in turn will ensure that the United States will remain disassociated with the negative connotations surrounding accusations of genocidal activities.

The significance of this work illustrates the need for military leadership at all levels of war to be familiar with the term, how to recognize the patterns that result in genocidal activities, and how it might impact mission accomplishment. As ambassadors of our Nation, military leaders must also understand United States history as it influences

---

[84] William Blum, *Rogue State: A Guide to the World's Only Superpower* (Monroe: Common Courage Press, 2000), 68-69.

the perception of our government as viewed from foreign nations. Lastly, by understanding genocide, future military leaders will be able to conduct and articulate the purpose of operations throughout the spectrum of warfare while remaining disassociated with accusations of genocide.

BIBLIOGRAPHY

Axelrod, Alan. *Chronicle of the Indian Wars Colonial Times to Wounded Knee.* New York: Prentice Hall General Reference, 1993.

American Officials Charged For War Crimes. http://www.thewinds.org/1997/02/war_crimes.html, accessed 01 March 2002.

American State Papers, Documents, Legislative and Executive, of the Congress of the United *States for the Second Session of the Twenty-Fourth, and First and Second Sessions of the Twenty-Fifth Congress, Commencing March 1, 1837 and Ending march 1, 1838.* Washington: Gales & Seaton, 1861.

Blum, William. *Rogue State: A Guide to the World's Only Superpower.* Monroe: Common Courage Press, 2000.

Charney, Israel W. *How Can We Commit the Unthinkable? Genocide: The Human Cancer.* Boulder: Westview Press, Inc., 1982.

Churchill, Ward. *A Little Matter Of Genocide*: *Holocaust and Denial in the Americas, 1492 to the Present.* San Fransico: City Lights Books, 1997.

Debo, Angie. *And Still the Waters Run: The Betrayal Of The Five Civilized Tribes.* Princeton: Princeton University Press, 1972.

Donaher, William F. and Ross B. Deblois. "Is the Current UN and US Policy toward Iraq Effective?," Parameters: US Army War College Quarterly 31, no. 4 (Winter 2001-02): 112-125.

Ehle, John. *Trail of Tears: The Rise And Fall Of The Cherokee Nation.* New York: Doubleday, a division of Bantam Doubleday Dell Publishing Group, Inc., 1988.

Lemkin, Ralph. "Genocide - A Modern Crime," Free World (New York), Vol. 9, No. 4, April 1945, http://www.preventgenocide.org/lemkin/freeworld1945.htm, accessed 12 December 2001.

Mankiller, Wilma and Michael Wallis. *Mankiller: A Chief and Her People.* Knoxville: University of Tennessee Press, 1979.

McLoughlin, William G. *After the Trail Of Tears: The Cherokees' Struggle For Sovereignty 1839-1880.* Chapel Hill: The University of North Carolina Press, 1993.

Stannard, David E. *American Holocaust: The Conquest of the New World.* New York: Oxford University Press, 1992.

Prucha, Francis Paul. *Documents of United States Indian Policy.* 3rd ed. Lincoln and London: University of Nebraska Press, 2000.

The Cherokee Indian Nation: A Troubled History. Ed. Duane H. King. Knoxville: The Tennessee University Press, 1979.

Thorton, Russell. *The Cherokees: A Population History*. Lincoln and London: University of Nebraska Press, 1992.

United Nations General Assembly. 1st session. Sixth Committee. *Summary Record of the 55th Plenary Meeting: Resolution on Genocide*. 11 December 1946. Official Record.

United Nations General Assembly. 3rd session. Sixth Committee. *Adoption of the Convention on the Prevention and Punishment of the Crime of Genocide*. 9 December 1948. Official Record.

Utley, Robert M. and Wilcomb E. Washburn. *Indian Wars*. New York: American Heritage Press, Inc., 1985.

Utter, Jack. *American Indians: Answers to Today's Questions*. Lake Ann: National Woodlands Publishing Company, 1993.

Wissler, Clark. *Indians of the United States*. Garden City: Doubleday & Company, Inc., 1966.

www.ingramcontent.com/pod-product-compliance
Lightning Source LLC
Chambersburg PA
CBHW081754280526
45789CB00008B/2848